Original title:
Orbiting Odes

Copyright © 2025 Creative Arts Management OÜ
All rights reserved.

Author: Gabriel Kingsley
ISBN HARDBACK: 978-1-80567-767-3
ISBN PAPERBACK: 978-1-80567-888-5

Celestial Dances

Planets twirl in disco lights,
But bumping heads? Oh, what a fright!
Stars giggle while they spin,
A cosmic show, let's begin!

Comets race on roller skates,
They're late again for cosmic dates!
Asteroids play tag, watch them slide,
In this vast, galactic ride!

Stardust Symphonies

The sun plays tunes on solar strings,
While Jupiter raps about its rings!
Mars drops beats like a DJ pro,
While Mercury dances fast, oh no!

Saturn swings with a wobbly grace,
Rings like hula hoops, they embrace!
Pluto mumbles, feeling left out,
While stars giggle and dance about!

Ethereal Journeys

Spaceships filled with snacks and dreams,
Zooming past in cosmic beams.
Aliens wave from starry lanes,
Offering ice cream that never wanes!

Galaxies twist with silly glee,
Playing hide and seek—come find me!
Nebulae swirl in colorful flares,
Sharing secrets with the moon's zany stares!

Twilight's Lullaby

Stars yawn softly, closing their eyes,
While the moon tells jokes in disguise.
Planets snicker as they drift,
In twilight's embrace, all spirits lift!

The heavens hum a cheeky tune,
While meteors wiggle, wishing for June.
Each constellation, a giggly friend,
In this cosmic lullaby, let the fun never end!

Interstellar Harmonies

In the void, a sock drifts free,
Spinning tales of laundry spree.
Stars chuckle, while comets dance,
Gravity's just a funny chance.

Aliens smile with greenish glee,
Trading jokes with a cup of tea.
Planets wobble in silly ways,
Creating laughs for light years' days.

Stellar Notes

A walrus plays the cosmic flute,
While Pluto wears its fuzzy suit.
Saturn's rings just like to swing,
As galaxies burst into a fling.

Quasars wink and laugh aloud,
While asteroids form a silly crowd.
Dancing light-years, they unite,
Creating tunes that feel just right.

Distant Worlds' Poetry

On Mars, a cactus wrote a guide,
On how to surf the stellar tide.
Venus giggles, "You guys are nuts!"
As she eats her spacey donuts!

The moon howls jokes that make you cheer,
While meteorites sip root beer.
In cosmic bars, puns take flight,
Under twinkling starlit night.

Cosmic Reflections

Black holes twirl in comedic flair,
While galaxies weave a perfect stare.
Stardust sneezes, a glittery spray,
As cosmic dust bunnies come out to play.

Asteroids jest, "We're just rocks!,"
As laughter bounces off moon blocks.
In the universe, fun finds its way,
Leaving smiles on planets that sway.

Astral Dances

In a tutu made of stardust bright,
Planets twirl in the cosmic night.
Jupiter's shoes are far too wide,
While Saturn's rings are quite the ride.

The comets skate with tails so long,
Doing the cha-cha, they feel so strong.
Mars tries the moonwalk, trips and slips,
While Venus giggles, twirling in flips.

Echoes in the Milky Way

Whispers bounce from star to star,
Silly stories of a cosmic car.
A black hole sneezes, oh what a sound,
While aliens laugh, spinning round and round.

Galaxies shout with a hearty cheer,
Starry pranks that tickle the ear.
A nebula winks, gives a bright glare,
As asteroids crash with a goofy flair.

Cosmic Enchantment

A celestial jester tells a joke,
While meteors giggle and gently poke.
Gravity laughs, pulling all in tight,
As moons play hide-and-seek, what a sight!

The sun throws a party with rays so bold,
While space dust dances, never gets old.
Jupiter's band rocks the stellar scene,
As aliens groove in their vibrant green.

Starlit Pathways

Under the stars, a pathway glows,
With twinkling lights where laughter flows.
A rocket ship sings a silly tune,
While the Earth spins 'neath a chubby moon.

Shooting stars race, in a friendly fight,
Leaving trails of glittering light.
A cosmic parade, full of cheer,
As the universe chuckles for all to hear.

Luminary Harmonics

Stars sing tunes from afar,
Comets dance like a bizarre.
Planets bump in a clumsy waltz,
Galaxies twirl, spinning with faults.

In the vastness, whoops and laughs,
Black holes munch on cosmic wafts.
A rogue asteroid slips on a shoe,
And moons giggle, 'What's that you do?'

Trails of the Wandering Comets

A comet's tail flips like a cat,
It sneezes sparkles, just like that!
Meteors fall like candy rain,
While stars play hopscotch, feeling no pain.

Planets fashion silly hats,
Mercury says, 'I'm too fast for chats!'
Venus teases with frilly flare,
While Saturn's rings spiral in the air.

Whirls of Celestial Joy

In the cosmos, we catch a break,
Orbits wobble like they're on cake.
Asteroids are often overzealous,
Playing tag, being quite rebellious.

Neptune giggles in shades of blue,
Says, 'Catch me if you think you knew!'
While Jupiter dances with a puff,
And whispers, 'Is this cosmic stuff?'

Echoes in the Night Sky

Stars chuckle and flash a grin,
As the moon dives for a spin.
Constellations strike a pose,
'Look at us, we're quite the pros!'

Satellites, like jesters, roam,
Finding the perfect place for home.
Uranus blushes in twilight's glow,
Saying, 'I'm the coolest, don't you know?'

Cosmic Embrace

I met a star with a wink and a grin,
Said, 'Quasars are chasing, let the fun begin!'
They danced through the void with a shake and a twist,
While black holes cheered, 'We can't resist!'

Aliens laughed in their silly green suits,
Playing space hopscotch with cosmic cute boots.
They flipped through the galaxies, giggling away,
In a universe where pranks rule the day!

Pulsar Rhythms

A pulsar was tapping its little bright feet,
Creating a dance that was funky and sweet.
The comets all joined with a spin and a bounce,
Making space boogie, you'd never pronounce!

With meteors flying like confetti galore,
They twirled in the nebula, asking for more.
Each beat from the stars made the planets all sway,
Joking 'Let's party 'til the Milky Way's gray!'

Dreaming in Starlight

In a dream where the stardust sprinkles about,
The moon told a joke, and the sun laughed out loud.
Planets spun slowly, their faces aglow,
As they shared silly secrets only they know.

A comet with glasses recited a pun,
"You'll never believe how we had so much fun!"
The cosmos erupted in giggles and glee,
While Saturn made funny faces for tea!

Universe's Serenade

The universe sang a delightful refrain,
With star notes that tickled like a gentle rain.
Galaxies whirled in a cacophony bright,
As they chuckled at Saturn's peculiar sight.

Distant stars twinkled with mischievous flair,
Telling space tales that twisted the air.
They joked about comets who wear silly hats,
While supernovae giggled like playful cats!

Gravity's Gentle Pull

In a cosmic dance, we float and swirl,
Chasing our dreams, like a dizzying whirl.
Planets giggle as they chase the sun,
Who knew space could be so much fun?

Stars winking down, like old pals in jest,
Throwing stardust, they know we're the best.
Each comet's tail is a party hat,
As we twirl in space like a playful cat.

Celestial Melodies in Motion

Jupiter's tune is a bouncy beat,
While Saturn's rings make the dance floor neat.
Venus sings sweetly in a velvet night,
While Mars tries to groove, but falls, what a sight!

Uranus chuckles, spinning on its side,
Neptune's all blue, but who's got the pride?
With every note, the galaxies sway,
In the symphony of space, we laugh and play.

The Quiet Dance of the Planets

Mercury zooms, the speedy little sprite,
While Earth takes its time, enjoying the night.
Venus twirls slowly, a ballerina fair,
A cosmic ballet, with stars everywhere.

Pluto's on the edge, giving a wave,
"I'm still in the game, look how I behave!"
Each planet's grace in the silent expanse,
In the quiet of space, we all love to dance.

Serenade of the Spheres

Sunshine beams in a curious way,
While the moons giggle, in their own ballet.
Pulsars pulse out a rhythm so bright,
And black holes just grin, out of pure delight.

Cosmic giggles echo through the night sky,
As meteors race on by with a sigh.
With laughter and joy, the stars all align,
In this wobbly waltz, everything's fine!

Cosmic Echo

In a galaxy full of cheese,
The stars do dance with such ease.
Planets spin on a giant plate,
But miss their flight, oh what a fate!

Asteroid belts make quite the mess,
Some call it space's great stress.
Comets streak with flashy tails,
While aliens trade their tall tales.

Supernova parties throw sparks,
As black holes munch on galactic parks.
Gravity plays a cosmic prank,
Pulling stars in a wild flank!

Through this vast and silly space,
Laughter echoes with each race.
So let us float with hearts so light,
In this comical starlit night!

Harmony of the Spheres

Notes of laughter fill the air,
As planets lift without a care.
Their tunes collide in joyful glee,
A cosmic band, come dance with me!

Mars hums low while Venus twirls,
Mercury zips with flips and swirls.
Jupiter joins with a thumping sound,
As rings of Saturn spin around!

Each celestial body sings its part,
Creating music straight from the heart.
Uranus chuckles with a sly grin,
While Neptune's sea breeze invites us in.

So let the universe play its song,
In this grand dance where we all belong.
A symphony of stars above,
Sharing laughter, sweetness, and love!

Lights Beyond the Horizon

Twinkling lights dance like fireflies,
In the vastness, they tease our eyes.
A shooting star winks with delight,
As we ponder who's out tonight!

In the shadows of the moon's glow,
We dream of voyages, high and low.
Martians giggle, making a fuss,
While space cats lounge on cosmic buses!

Galaxies swirl in vibrant hues,
While space pirates sing the blues.
With telescopes, we spy and peek,
At aliens that squeak and squeak!

Journeying through this stellar show,
With laughter trailing, off we go!
Beyond the horizon, joy we'll find,
In the vastness, we're all aligned!

Celestial Harmonies

In the sky, stars play tag,
Planets wobble with a brag.
When comets race, they leave a trail,
While meteorites proclaim their hail.

Saturn spins with its ringed flair,
Uranus laughs, 'Oh, what a dare!'
Mars will boast its rusty hue,
While Venus sways — oh, look at you!

Universe's Breath

Galaxies twist in a dance,
Some star systems take a chance.
Neptune's winds, a playful tease,
Dropping bars like cosmic bees.

Black holes munch with a loud slurp,
While asteroids give a little burp.
Stars gossip in radiant light,
Filling the void with quirks of night.

Void's Melodies

Shooting stars play hide and seek,
While aliens tickle the cheek.
Cosmic dust floats like confetti,
"Get your space snacks!" they cry, all ready.

Pluto pouts, "Too far from games!",
While Jupiter jests, "I'm not to blame!"
Satellites share their funny memes,
Cosmic comedy in starry dreams!

Echoes of the Cosmos

Saturn swings with a grin so wide,
Even Neptune jokes with pride.
Galactic tales wrapped in light,
Who knew space could be so bright?

Starships zoom with candy wraps,
While quasars throw the best of naps.
Cosmic beats make meteors sway,
In this strange, whimsical ballet!

Harmonies of the Astral Winds

In a galaxy far, far away,
Stars hum tunes in a playful sway.
Planets wear hats of cotton candy,
Dancing in rhythm, oh so dandy.

A comet spills secrets with a grin,
While black holes chuckle, sucking in.
Meteor showers throw a wild bash,
With twinkling lights, they really splash!

Dreaming in the Milky Way

Floating on stardust, no cares tonight,
Galactic giggles take off in flight.
Nebulae painted in bubblegum hues,
Tickle our senses, like popcorn chew.

Aliens roast marshmallows with flair,
Sipping starlight from a cosmic chair.
Creatures cryptic with a wink in their eye,
Wave as we pass, oh my, oh my!

Waltzing with the Cosmos

Planets pirouette in a cosmic ball,
Twinkling stars jest, 'Are we too small?'
Saturn wears rings that jingle with glee,
While Uranus jokes, 'Just look at me!'

Dance on the asteroids, twirl in the void,
Gravity's rules just a little toy.
Galaxies whisper sweet nothings at night,
As laughter ignites with the soft starlight.

Notes from a Cosmic Canvas

Brushstrokes of starlight paint the skies,
Comets create mischief, oh what a surprise!
A canvas of chaos, a masterful fun,
Galactic laughter, never overdone.

Shooting stars sketch doodles, it's true,
While planets explore the universe blue.
Every twinkle a giggle, every shine a jest,
In this grand masterpiece, we are all blessed!

Celestial Whispers

In the night sky stars do twinkle,
Planets spin with a little wrinkle.
Mars winks at Venus, what a sight,
While Saturn shows off its ring so tight.

Comets dash by with a whoosh,
Shooting stars, oh what a push!
Luna's giggles bounce on the breeze,
Making asteroids laugh with ease.

Jupiter's storms are quite the show,
Swirling chaos in a cosmic flow.
Are those cosmic cats chasing tails?
Now that's a mystery that never fails.

Galaxies swirl in a pillow fight,
Stardust pillows through the night.
While black holes snicker, "Round we go,"
In the vastness, fun's the only flow.

Spheres of Silent Serenades

The sun's a drummer, beating loud,
While moons gather, forming a crowd.
Saturn claps with its rings all bold,
As the space band plays, stories unfold.

Planets take turns on a merry-go-round,
Mars trips over, tumbles down, oh sound!
Pluto sits out, pouting away,
"I can be fun, please let me play!"

Moons dance around, a jolly parade,
With a mix of waltz and a little charade.
Stars laugh together, glowing so bright,
As constellations hug them tight.

Meteor showers rain down confetti,
Making wishes, all warm and sweaty.
In this cosmic dance, all is fair,
Galactic giggles fill the air.

Eclipsed in Reverie

A moonlit dance, such a tease,
When sun and moon tango with ease.
They play peekaboo; the whole world gapes,
As shadows prance in funny shapes.

The sun says, "Hey, you missed a step!"
The moon, with laughter, gives a pep.
A little cloud drifts by to say,
"Don't forget, it's time to play!"

Star clusters cheer with sparkly flair,
Whispers bounce off the cosmic air.
Bright twinkling tales of giggly fights,
As dreams float freely in the night.

Finally, the show must end, oh dear,
As stars catch their breath and disappear.
But in the silence, giggles remain,
Echoing softly, sweet cosmic refrain.

Dance of the Heavenly Bodies

Planets pirouette, a flashy affair,
Jupiter jumps high; it's out of its chair.
Saturn spins 'round, what a sight to see,
While Neptune chuckles, "Look at me!"

Comets glide past with a whoosh and a swirl,
Making orbits dizzy, oh what a whirl!
Stars in the back rows are laughing out loud,
As meteors dance, forming a crowd.

Uranus winks, looking quite sly,
"Who knew space could be so spry?"
Stars twirl and leap in a cosmic ballet,
Making up moves as they dance away.

The galaxies party, shining so bright,
In the cosmic gloom, they are the light.
With every giggle, the universe grows,
In this wacky waltz, anything goes.

Night Sky's Lament

Why do stars always twinkle?
Are they just blinking at us?
A cosmic game of hide and seek,
 Or simply a starlit fuss?

Planets spinning with no care,
Hiding behind the moon's face.
Do they know how silly they look,
In this vast and endless space?

Comets zooming with tails ablaze,
Leaving trails of glittering crumbs.
Do they giggle as they fly past?
Or just enjoy the vibrant hums?

Shooting stars make wishes with glee,
But who grants them in the dark?
Are there cosmic wish-granters too,
 Sipping stardust from a spark?

Infinite Voyages

Rockets zooming through the void,
With snacks packed for the ride.
Do astronauts play tag up there?
Or is all the fun they hide?

Asteroids bounce like rubber balls,
Making music, what a sight!
Do they dance around in circles?
Singing songs to the night?

Planets argue over who's best,
Mars says he's the strongest guy.
Jupiter just laughs with glee,
While Saturn rings in a sly goodbye.

Galaxies swirl in a daze,
Trading secrets with a twist.
Do they gossip with their moons,
About stardust that they missed?

Celestial Whirl

The sun wears shades, it's quite a look,
Winking at us like a book.
Do planets stop to take a peek,
At this bold star, so subtle and sleek?

Saturn spins with flair and style,
While Jupiter just cracks a smile.
Do they have a fashion show?
Or hide behind celestial glow?

Stars throw parties, can't you see?
Shooting confetti, wild and free.
Do galaxies join in the fun,
Or just spin circles until they run?

Black holes laugh, a cosmic joke,
Swallowing light, they like to poke.
Do they chuckle, feeling sly,
As we wonder, "Where'd that star fly?"

Astronomical Tales

Once a comet wore a hat,
Too big for its small, icy head.
It tripped and fell in space so wide,
Leaving stardust where it's led.

A moon once claimed to be the best,
Boasted brighter than the rest.
But the sun just chuckled loud,
Saying, "Honey, that's a jest!"

Galaxies meet for a coffee break,
Swapping stories of their aches.
Do they laugh at distant stars,
And the silly shapes that it makes?

Aliens trade their cosmic memes,
In a world of shimmering beams.
Do they giggle at our silly ways,
As they zoom through dreamy dreams?

Gravity's Embrace

In a dance, I trip and fall,
Like a marble in a hall.
I'm pulled down by Mother Earth,
She laughs at my clumsy mirth.

I float like a feathered bird,
Yet gravity makes me absurd.
I try to leap with all my might,
But end up flat, what a sight!

I chase my hat caught in the breeze,
Falling down, oh, such unease.
With every tumble, giggles rise,
I swear I'm training for the skies!

Lunar Serenade

Under the moon, my shoes go clomp,
The shadows dance, the crickets chomp.
I moonwalk with a swanky flair,
But trip on rocks, oh, not so rare.

A rocket ship made from tin foil,
My buddies laugh, it's all in toil.
I'm off to seek the cheese that's there,
But tumble wide, it's all not fair!

My special dance makes the stars chuckle,
As I land with a grand old shuffle.
The moon beams down in silver glow,
While my moves steal the cosmic show!

Cosmic Cadence

In the dark, I spin and twirl,
My dance moves give the star dust swirl.
I add a twist, then bop, then sway,
The universe joins in my play.

I think I'm sleek, a starry dancer,
But I've got two left feet, a prancer!
Though meteors dodge my flailing arms,
They can't resist my goofy charms.

Around the sun, I trip around,
Applauding myself with every sound.
Galaxies laugh, they know my plight,
But I keep jigging through the night!

Solar Rhapsody

I swim in rays like silly fish,
But usually I crash, oh my wish!
With solar flares, I try to groove,
But my rhythm's not meant to prove.

These sunbeams tickle as I prance,
Yet here I land, without a chance.
I bump and roll, all in good cheer,
A solar system—a dancing sphere!

Chasing shadows down a sunbeam,
I slip and slide, not as it seems.
With every leap, I laugh and sway,
Making sunshine games my way!

Phases of Light

As I spin in circles, head in a twirl,
The moon shouts, 'Hey, stop making me swirl!'
Stars giggle softly, lighting the night,
While comets take selfies, what a silly sight.

I tried to dance with a nearby star,
But ended up tripping—oh, how bizarre!
Light beams are laughing, they twist and shout,
'You call that a tango? We've gotta bounce out!'

Planets are rolling, each one a prank,
Jupiter's wearing a silly old tank.
Saturn's rings wobble, they sway and fall,
Galactic chaos, a cosmic free-for-all.

So join the party, let laughter ignite,
In the cosmic dance, all's merry and bright.
With winks from the heavens, jokes seen from afar,
Life's a grand jesture—next stop, bizarre!

Galactic Murmurs

In the void, where whispers twirl,
Galaxies giggle, how they unfurl.
A neutron star jokes, 'Can you take a nap?'
While black holes cackle, 'It's a cosmic trap!'

Asteroids race like kids on a spree,
'Catch us if you can!' they laugh with glee.
Meteor showers bring tales to delight,
As space dust sprinkles on the endless night.

Supernovae burst, all colors abound,
'Look at me shining, I'm the biggest around!'
While aliens chuckle with popcorn in hand,
Watching the drama unfold, oh so grand.

Let's toast to the chaos, the fun in the void,
In stellar antics, we're all overjoyed.
Life's simple pleasures, louche and absurd,
Galactic giggles, forever unheard.

Cosmic Love Letters

In the vastness, I pen with starlight bright,
Love notes to planets, oh what a sight!
Dear Venus, you're lovely, with beauty unmatched,
But Mars just replied, 'I'm a little detached.'

In my heart-shaped orbit, love's a big joke,
Whispers of passion from the sunbeam folk.
The moons all conspire, with hearts in their glow,
'Venus and Mars? A celestial show!'

Each quasar twinkles, a wink from afar,
'I think you two are just cosmic bizarre.'
But love's not a race, it's a whirl and a spin,
Through galaxies far, let the laughter begin!

So here's to the stardust that we all share,
In my letters of love, there's whimsical flair.
To you from infinity, with humor so sweet,
In this galaxy of giggles, my heart finds its beat!

Solar Flare Fantasies

A burst of laughter, the sun explodes,
Solar flares dancing in dazzling codes.
They wiggle and jiggle, a fiery game,
While planets chuckle, calling out names.

Mercury quips, 'I'm too hot to stand!'
While Venus rolls eyes, 'I'm burned out, man.'
Earth's dancing wildly, in beautiful sway,
While Moons are all laughing, the fun's here to stay.

A solar picnic, with comets as guests,
Making wishes on streams, they're all such jest.
Each flicker of brightness, a jest in the sky,
While the universe winks, oh my oh my!

So, join the sun's party, in cosmic ballet,
See laughter ignite in the Milky Way.
With flares shooting joy, pure, unrestrained,\nIn this wacky solar play, we all are entertained!

Luminary Lullabies

In the sky, a lightbulb glows,
Winking down as night bestows.
Stars giggle with twinkling cheer,
Dance to dreams that draw us near.

A moonbeam rides a comet's tail,
Chasing shadows on a whale.
Clouds fluff up like cotton candy,
Sweetening nights, oh so dandy!

Shooting stars play hide and seek,
Whisp'ring secrets, strong yet meek.
They tell tales of cosmic pranks,
As they zoom above the banks.

Each night a comic show unfolds,
With laughter in the starlit molds.
Celestial jesters take a bow,
Leaving us in giggles now!

Heavenly Cadences

The sun hops up on a pogo stick,
Juggling planets, what a trick!
Venus giggles, dressed in pink,
While Mars pretends to not blink.

Saturn spins its hula hoop,
While Neptune joins a dancing troop.
Uranus laughs with a cheeky grin,
As the cosmos starts to spin.

A meteor takes a silly fall,
Knocking laughter from us all.
The Milky Way sings a funny song,
Inviting everyone along.

Galactic gales of giggled sighs,
Painting joy across the skies.
With every wink of a star's beam,
The universe flows as a dream!

Starlight Narratives

A star told tales of silly fears,
Of cosmic socks and forgotten cheers.
Nebulas wrapped in rainbow wraps,
While suns played cards and made mishaps.

The black hole threw a wild party,
Inviting all, both loud and hearty.
Gravity tried to step on toes,
As planets laughed in funny rows.

Comets raced, a wild parade,
With trails of sparkles in cascade.
Old asteroids shared their woes,
Recalling when they wore pink bows.

In the night, a large surprise,
A supernova with glittery eyes.
They danced around till break of dawn,
Singing songs that go on and on!

Celestial Nocturne

The moon plays tricks with a sly grin,
While stars chuckle, their lights spin.
Jupiter wears a silly hat,
Claiming it's just a new cool cat.

Lunar beams slide on cosmic skates,
While asteroids share their dinner plates.
"Pass the stars!" a small comet squeaks,
As laughter echoes through the peaks.

Galaxies whirl like a ballroom dance,
Twinkling in some cosmic romance.
A meteorite bumps and crashes loud,
Breaking up the starlit crowd.

With every blink and every jest,
The universe finds joy and rest.
In the night, with a wink of light,
The cosmos brings pure delight!

Cosmic Lullabies

Close your eyes, the stars will hum,
A dance of planets, look, here they come.
Jupiter juggles while Saturn does spins,
Comets throw parties with old cosmic twins.

Mars tells jokes, all about his red hue,
While Venus and Earth laugh, oh so true.
Neptune's got secrets, a laugh so absurd,
In this celestial gathering, no words are unheard.

Galaxies giggle, black holes just chortle,
A space-time circus, with a cosmic throttle.
Gravity's winks as it pulls at your feet,
In this starry playground, there's joy that's sweet.

So drift off to dreams where the comets all play,
In these cosmic lullabies, you'll float away.
With starlight above, and the moon's gentle sway,
Embrace all the laughter, come join in the fray.

Stardust Sonnet

In the night sky, a giggle erupts,
Planets in jest, oh how they disrupt!
Mercury teases with fast little zips,
While moons share tales of those cosmic trips.

An asteroid chuckles, a rock with a grin,
Winking at Earth, where the fun can begin.
Galaxies swirl in a wild, bright spree,
Painting the canvas, hilarious and free.

Neptune's a joker, his humor quite blue,
While Pluto, the outcast, still feels part of the crew.
Stars sparkle with laughter, as comets collide,
In this wondrous theater, where giggles abide.

So laugh with the stars, and forget all your woes,
In this stardust sonnet, joy endlessly flows.
With each cosmic chuckle, your heart will take flight,
As the universe dances and twinkles with light.

Round and Round in Grace

Planets pirouette, oh what a sight,
With suns that twinkle, they're dancing in light.
Mercury spins with its dizzying pace,
While Venus just twirls, with elegant grace.

Uranus rolls over, a tumble so grand,
Jupiter's laughter is easy to understand.
As Neptune spins tales with a mystical air,
The cosmos delights in this whimsical fair.

Black holes may grumble, they hoard all the fun,
But stars share glimmers for everyone.
Each meteoric leap, a joyride in space,
In this round and round, every heart finds its place.

So join in the swirl, let your worries unwind,
In laughter's embrace, leave your troubles behind.
With gravity's pull, we all dance in trance,
Round and round we go, lost in this cosmic romance.

Gravity's Embrace

Falling for laughter, it's all in the game,
The universe chuckles, it's never the same.
Stars pull in close, like a warm, fuzzy hug,
As meteors tumble, they dance like a bug.

Planets play tag in a whimsical race,
Comets fly by, with a cheeky little face.
Celestial bodies perform on a whim,
In a dance with gravity, no need to be prim.

Earth spins a yarn, a tale that is light,
While the moon chuckles softly, glowing at night.
The cosmos conspires to tickle your soul,
In gravity's embrace, we all feel whole.

So let's share some giggles as we drift through the space,
In this joyful ballet, find your special place.
With laughter as stardust, we float in delight,
In gravity's arms, every moment feels right.

Comet's Kiss

A comet swoops by with a wink,
It steals my heart in a blink.
I called out, "Hey, don't pass me by!"
But it just laughed, saying, "Oh my!"

With tails that sparkle like sprightly stars,
It zooms around, leaving no scars.
I waved my hands, hoping for more,
But that cheeky comet just soared out the door!

It kissed the sun with a fiery grin,
Shooting chocolates instead of gin.
I took a chance, I threw a wish,
And caught a donut in my dish!

So here I sit beneath the night,
With snacks in hand, my heart feels light.
While comets fly by, in a playful race,
I'll munch my treats with a smile on my face.

Ecliptic Dreams

In dreams I slide on a cosmic sphere,
Riding stardust, nothing to fear.
My cat's an astronaut, with boots and a hat,
While dancing moons say, "Look at that!"

We spin 'round planets like crazy fools,
In space, we ignore all the rules.
With pizza rockets and soda springs,
We rule the cosmos—oh, what fun it brings!

Then suddenly, my dreams go dark,
Was that my alarm or a shooting spark?
I wake to find I'm still in my bed,
Crazy ecliptic dreams dance in my head!

But when I close my eyes once more,
I'm back in space, I laugh and soar.
I'll skip through stars with my feline friend,
In these funny dreams, there's no end.

Moonbeam Melodies

Moonbeams twirl and dance with glee,
They sing a tune just for me.
My walls hum back with a silly face,
And join the party in outer space!

With light as soft as a cotton ball,
We bounce around in a cosmic hall.
The universe plays jazz, oh so fine,
While I moonwalk on the Milky Way line!

A space raccoon lends me his hat,
He says, "Let's jam, don't be a brat!"
Together we create a rhythmic show,
With comets tapping feet down below.

As stars applaud with twinkling cheers,
I waltz 'round planets, conquering fears.
In moonbeam melodies, I will sway,
Laughing with joy, come what may!

Spacebound Soliloquies

Floating through thoughts of light and cheer,
I chat with stars that glisten near.
They giggle and wink, and share their tales,
Of misadventures in cosmic gales.

I ask a black hole how it feels,
It just smiles, stealing my meals!
"Bring me your snacks, they'll disappear,
Where I go, there's nothing here!"

In rocket-powered shoes, I prance,
While asteroid rocks join in the dance.
With each silly twist and harmless twirl,
I become the universe's dancing girl!

But even in laughter, I ponder why,
Do space bunnies bounce, or just float by?
In spacebound soliloquies, I muse,
While giggles echo—the infinite fuse!

The Spiral Symphony

In circles we dance, oh what a sight,
Planets with pizza, a cosmic delight!
Saturn's rings shimmer, they're quite the show,
While asteroids wiggle in a galactic glow.

With meteors racing, they're late to the game,
Chasing their tails, oh the stars feel the same!
Galaxies giggle, as they spin round and round,
In the vastness of space, fun's always found.

Aliens peek out, with their eyes big and wide,
In search of a snack on this cosmic ride!
While comets bring cookies, trailing sweet dust,
In this jolly ballet, laughter's a must!

The moon grins brightly, in a cheeky prank,
Creating a ruckus with stars on a plank!
With each twinkling wink, a joke is revealed,
In this spiral symphony, joy is sealed.

Celestial Songs from Afar

From beyond the clouds, a tune drifts in,
Comets are crooning, oh what a din!
Mars joins in boldly, with his rusty groove,
While Venus spins softly, trying to move.

Galactic guitars strum stardust stones,
Satellites dance, shaking their phones!
Jupiter leaps, with a swing and a dip,
He's got the rhythm, can't let it slip!

With harmonious swirls, the nebulae sway,
Singing for Earth, what a marvelous play!
While meteors tap dance in stylish flair,
In this grand concert, fun's everywhere!

Each star's a note, in a cosmic chorus,
Galaxies harmonize, just for us!
As space winks and twirls, a humor parade,
In the celestial songs, adventures are made.

Between the Stars and Us

Between the stars, oh what a tease,
Whispers of aliens, 'Want some cheese?'
Rockets zoom past with a honk and a beep,
While stardust giggles, they just can't keep.

Floating along, like fish in a stream,
In this cosmic circus, it's all a dream!
Aliens juggle with gravity's grace,
While the sun gives a wink, lighting up space.

Little asteroids rock in a band,
Making a ruckus, while flying so grand!
Comets do cartwheels in their comet suits,
Playing with moons, in their funky boots.

A rift in the heavens, where laughter ignites,
With twinkling eyes, our joy takes flight!
Between the stars, let the fun expand,
In this quirky galaxy, together we stand.

Constellations of the Heart

Drawn in the sky, a whimsical map,
Constellations giggle, just like a chap!
Like winking stars with a secret to share,
They poke fun at Venus, with tales full of flair.

Big Dipper's spinning, oh what a churn,
As Cassiopeia gives a cheeky turn!
The stars throw a party, with laughter and light,
While the Milky Way twirls, pure delight!

Twirling meteors sing with glee,
As distant planets make a playful decree,
With hearts made of starlight, they join the dance,
Creating a rapture, a cosmic romance.

In this dazzling expanse, love and jest meet,
The constellations laugh, isn't life sweet?
With every twinkling hope that we see,
In the universe's embrace, we're wild and free!

Whirling Galaxies

In a swirl of stars, we dance at night,
Planets tumble around, what a sight!
Comets zoom by, with tails so bright,
Aliens wave from their land of delight.

Gravity giggles, pulling us near,
A space trampoline, have no fear!
Floating on laughter, a cosmic cheer,
We cartwheel through darkness, no need for a steer.

Rockets made of candy, oh what a treat,
Zooming past moons on candy floss feet.
Twinkling surprises in every heartbeat,
Galactic mischief, none can compete.

The Milky Way's gooey, like sweet taffy,
Stuck in the cosmos, aren't we all gaffy?
With each silly orbit, we giggle and chaffy,
In this wondrous circus, we're all quite happy.

Constellation Songs

Singing up high in the cosmic choir,
Stars hum a tune, taking us higher.
Planets join in, their voices conspire,
A melody bold that will never tire.

The bears and the dogs dance side by side,
A celestial jig on this galactic ride.
Orions' belt's got such a weird stride,
While Venus laughs, unable to hide.

Twinkle boxes float, bursting with sound,
Comet karaoke as laughter rebounds.
Shooting stars jump, landing all around,
In this star-studded fest, joy is profound.

Even the black holes hum tunes so deep,
While galaxies sway, no time for sleep.
In this stellar party, our dreams we keep,
Cosmic concerts, oh what treasures we reap!

Radiant Horizons

At dawn, the sun fuels a wild race,
Planetary pranks at a dizzying pace.
With morning's glow upon every face,
A hopscotch across the great outer space.

Rockets with sunglasses zoom through the rays,
While moons play tag in a luminous maze.
Light beams are wiggling, brightening days,
Caught in the sunshine, what fun displays!

Mercury dashes, the speedster supreme,
Saturn wears rings like a fancy dream.
Jupiter's giggles are loud as they seem,
In this radiant fun, we all join the team.

At twilight, the laughter drifts far and wide,
Planets spin tales on this cosmic ride.
As night comforts, let joy be our guide,
Through radiant horizons, together we glide.

Aetherial Chants

Whirling through space on a whimsic breeze,
Singing with aliens under the trees.
Nebulae bubbles, oh how they tease,
Comets chuckle, just like they please.

With starry shenanigans taking the stand,
Mars flips pancakes for the whole astral band.
They pour syrup moons from a great golden hand,
A feast in the cosmos, altogether we stand.

Aetherial chants in a flurry of laughs,
Uranus, the joker, just jests with the drafts.
Black holes are portals for cosmic drafts,
In this swirling realm, we dive into gaffes.

The universe giggles with playful delight,
Every planet's a character, whimsical sight.
Join us as we dance through the vibrant night,
In aetherial dreams, everything feels right.

Heavenly Rhapsody

Up in the sky, a cat in space,
Chasing stars at a worldly pace.
Comets zoom past, waving their tails,
While the moon steals cheese from the gales.

A planet winks and giggles loud,
Dancing on clouds, oh so proud.
Galaxies spin, doing a jig,
As asteroids groove, feeling quite big.

Stars throw a party, all dressed up bright,
Nebulas twirl in a glittering night.
Astro-bunnies hop with a spring,
While sleepy suns begin to sing.

The universe rolls, a cosmic jest,
In this grand show, we're all guests.
With a laugh and a cheer, join the ride,
In this stellar fun, let joy be your guide!

Timeless Circles of Light

Round and round goes the cosmic wheel,
Planets race on, oh what a deal!
Saturn's rings play jump rope with Mars,
While Venus throws stardust from her jars.

A comet's tail has quite the flair,
Dodging asteroids with a twist in the air.
The sun, a joker, beams a bright grin,
Saying, 'Let the space games begin!'

Galactic giggles echo so sweet,
As shooting stars dance on their feet.
Wormholes swirl in a giggly spree,
Who knew space could be so carefree?

Through timeless circles, the fun must flow,
In this cosmic carnival, come let's go!
With laughter that echoes, and joy so rife,
These timeless lights bring cosmic life!

Celestial Reveries

Dreamy planets in pajamas float,
In cosmic beds with stars that gloat.
Jupiter snores, while little moons hum,
Venus styles her celestial plum.

The Milky Way writes comic strips,
Galaxies giggle with comic quips.
Nebula clouds, all fluffy and bright,
Whispering secrets in the night light.

Aliens bake cosmic pies in the void,
While asteroids pass, feeling quite annoyed.
With cosmic sprinkles and starry glaze,
The universe shimmers in a playful daze.

Through celestial dreams, let laughter soar,
For in these reveries, we find much more.
In the tapestry woven of light and cheer,
These cosmic tales bring us all near!

Starlit Whispers

In the starlit night, giggles abound,
Comets with jokes spinning around.
A shooting star slips on a bright ray,
Saying, 'Oops! Have a wonderful day!'

The moon's a prankster, with shadows so sly,
Telling tales that make you laugh and cry.
Galaxies gather for a light-hearted chat,
Trading funny stories, where's the cat?

While planets spin tales of old,
In whispers of laughter, cosmic and bold.
With a wink from the sun, the fun never ends,
In starlit whispers, we dance with friends.

So if you find yourself lost in the night,
Join the celestial fun, hold on tight!
For in this vast cosmos, laughter takes flight,
In starlit whispers, everything feels right!

Whispers of the Universe

In space, they say, all things are neat,
Stars giggle softly, a cosmic tweet.
Planets twirl like kids at play,
In this grand dance, who leads the way?

Comets race with ice cream tails,
Jupiter rolls, and Saturn hails.
Galaxies spin like tops gone mad,
In this vast realm, you can't be sad!

Radio waves hum a silly tune,
Twirling moons under a cheese-shaped moon.
Asteroids dodge with a comic flare,
While black holes joke from their chair!

So listen close, with a cheeky grin,
The universe laughs, let the fun begin!
Each twinkle and spark, a goofy sight,
In this celestial giggle, all feels right.

Aether's Touch

A gentle breeze from the stars above,
Whispers of laughter, a cosmic glove.
Galactic hiccups, starry blunders,
Laughter echoes through space's wonders.

With comets chasing their own long tails,
And shooting stars sharing weird tales.
Venus flirts with Mars in jest,
While Earth munches popcorn, and says, "I'm blessed!"

Meteor showers fall, like candy sprinkles,
On a playground where no one crinkles.
The aether's touch is a playful tease,
In this dance of quirks, we aim to please!

So, twirl with the moons, take a silly leap,
Into the cosmos where laughter doesn't sleep!
Feel the aether's soft and funny nudge,
In this galactic gig, never judge!

Nebula's Kiss

Clouds of color in space's embrace,
Nebulas chuckle, swirling in grace.
With a pop and a sizzle, they play a game,
Creating stars, but never the same.

They twinkle and shimmer, with whimsical flair,
Like cosmic cupcakes in vibrant air.
Stardust sprinkles down, a sweet delight,
As planets burst forth in a dazzling light.

Galactic giggles dance through the night,
While comets high-five, it's quite the sight!
The universe sings songs of glee,
As nebulae wink at you and me.

So float on a whim, let your spirit soar,
In the clouds of color, we'll laugh some more!
For every day's a party in this vast abyss,
A playful touch from the nebula's kiss!

Celestial Streams

There's a river of stars, flowing so bright,
With laughter that tickles the endless night.
Planets splash in galactic spills,
While the sun bakes cookies on cosmic hills.

Comets swing by, with a "whoosh" and a grin,
Playing tag with the stardust, let the fun begin!
A black hole giggles, swallows it whole,
In this playful soup, we all have a role.

Shooting stars dive, making wishes galore,
As space dust dances, forevermore.
The universe flows in whimsical streams,
Where laughter bubbles up, and joy redeems.

So skip on the planets, make friends with the sun,
In this cosmic escape, together we run!
With each twinkle and laugh, let's make our mark,
In the celestial streams, where joy leaves a spark!

www.ingramcontent.com/pod-product-compliance
Lightning Source LLC
Chambersburg PA
CBHW071821160426
43209CB00003B/162